Mantises

Joi Washington

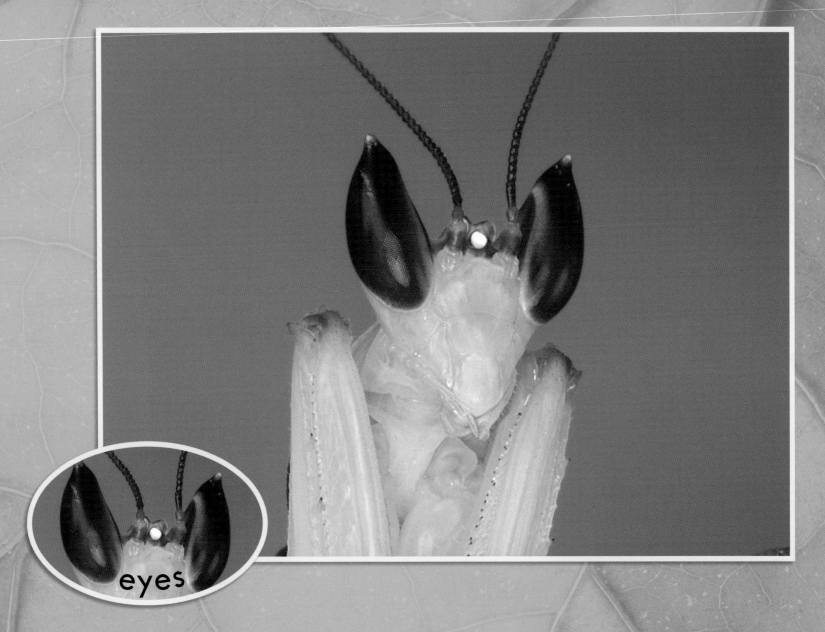

eyes

Do you see the mantis with the eyes?

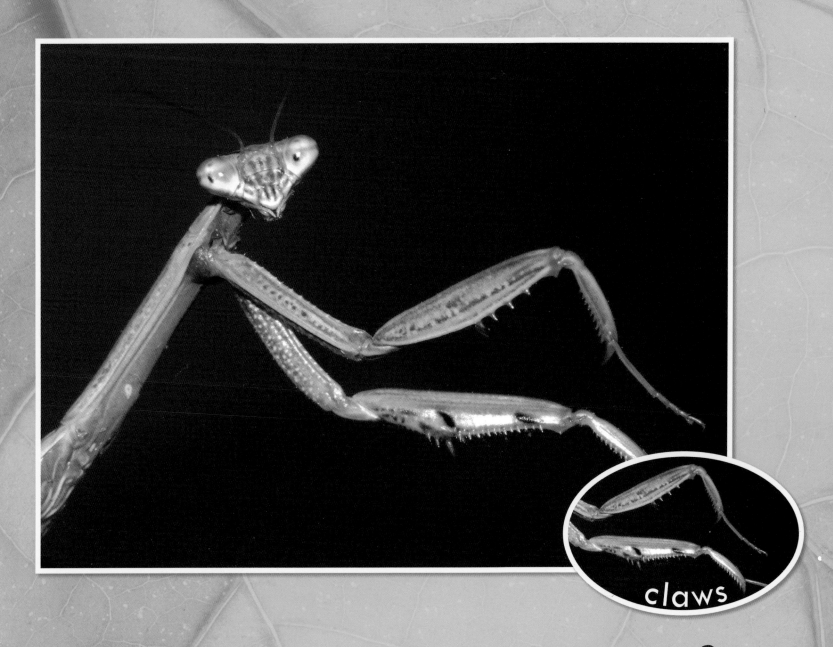

claws

Do you see the mantis with the claws?

3

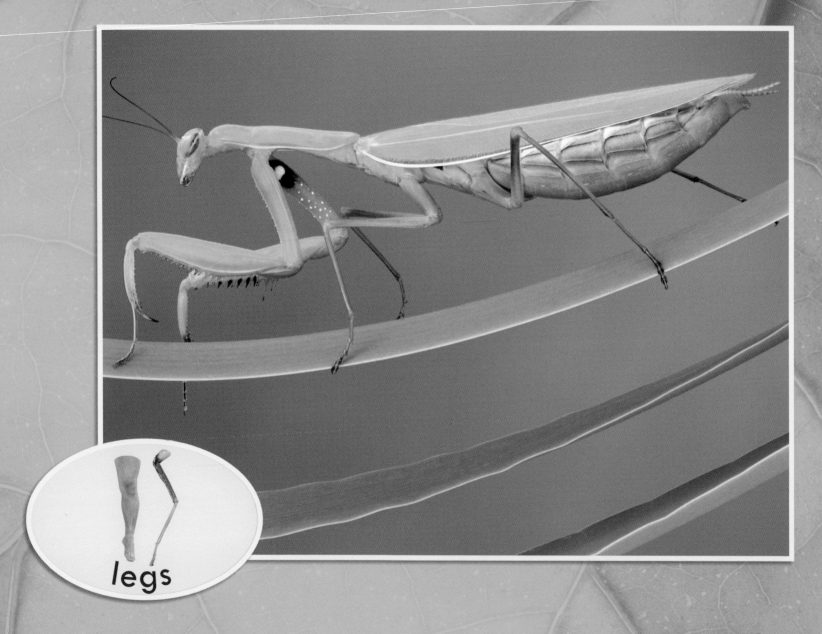

legs

Do you see the mantis with the legs?

wings

Do you see the mantis with the wings?

flower

Do you see the mantis with the flower?

6

leaf

Do you see the mantis with the leaf?

grass

Do you see the mantis with the grass?

8

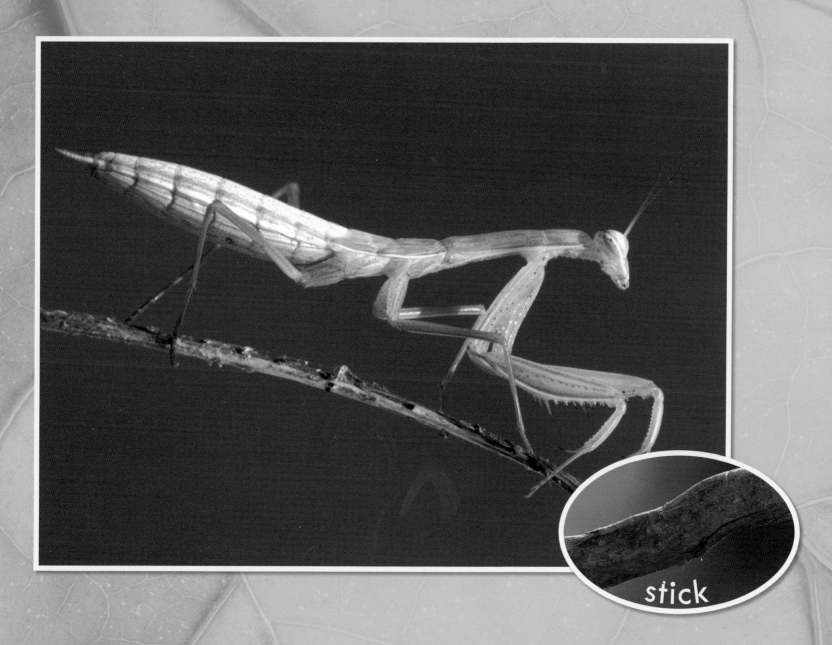

stick

Do you see the mantis with the stick?

rain

Do you see the mantis with the rain?

butterfly

Do you see the mantis with the butterfly?

grasshopper

Do you see the mantis with the grasshopper?

12

beetle

Do you see the mantis with the beetle?

13

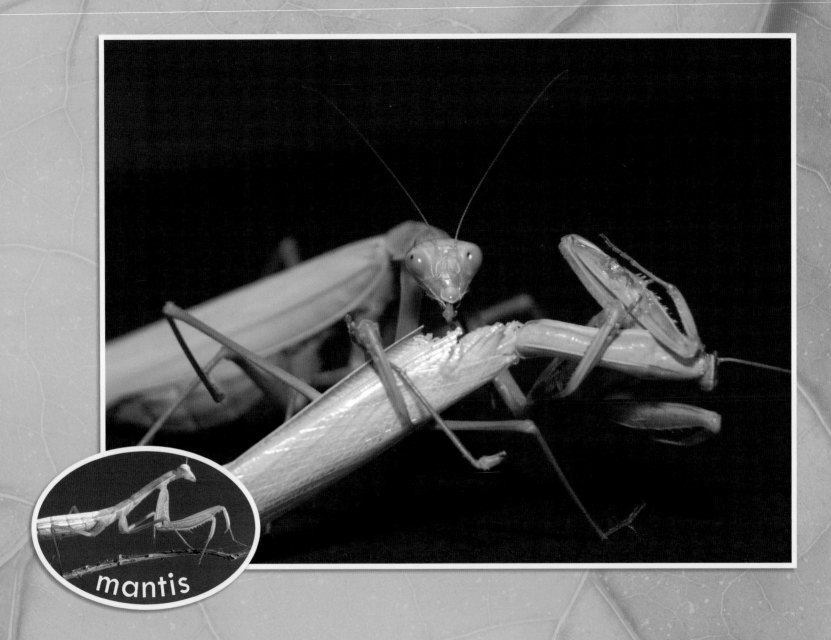

mantis

Do you see the mantis with the mantis?

lizard

Do you see the mantis with the lizard?

Do

do

you

see

the

with